St. Martin de Porres

St. Martin

de Porres

By His Eminence

Richard Cardinal Cushing

UT COGNOSCANT TE

ST. PAUL EDITIONS

Gratitude is expressed to Rev. Norbert Georges, O.P., Director of the St. Martin de Porres Guild, for illustrations used in this book.

Library of Congress Catalog Card Number: 62-20203

CONTENTS

Martin

De

Porres

THE

SAINT

On Sunday, May 6, 1962, His Holiness Pope John XXIII proclaimed—in the presence of thirty-eight Cardinals, many archbishops, prelates, diplomatic representatives of more than fifty countries and a throng of laity from every part of the globe—the sanctity of Martin de Porres. The news services of the world have spread far and wide the biographical data on this Dominican Brother, this brilliant star in the crown of the New World, this glory of Latin America.

Long before the day of canonization arrived, tickets for the ceremony were exhausted. Thousands of pilgrims from countries halfway around the globe poured into Rome to celebrate the official inscription of the 17th century Dominican lay Brother from Peru in the roll of officially declared saints.

The Vatican basilica never before was so brilliantly lighted. For the first time the vast church's completely renovated lighting system was switched on. An audible sigh of surprise and wonder welled up from the thousands inside the basilica when the lights from a thousand hidden nooks filled the shadowy reaches with splendor.

Packed into the boxes, tribunes and standing room areas surrounding the main sanctuary were three thousand pilgrims from Spain and a thousand from Peru. Fifteen hundred others came from Ireland, as well as hundreds from the United States, Chile, Ecuador, Brazil, South Africa, Trinidad and the Philippines.

From two great pillars supporting St. Peter's mighty dome hung huge paintings portraying the two miracles which were verified to support Martin's canonization. And close to the Pope's throne was a twelve-year-old boy from the Canary Islands, the subject of one of the paintings, who was cured of gangrene through St. Martin's intercession.

What are the salient characteristics of this new saint and what lessons are to be learned from his life?

The life of any saint is proof of the power of God's grace to overcome the weakness of human nature. In the life of St. Martin de Porres, we have an unusual manifestation of the combination of divine strength and human insufficiency. In this newly canonized servant of God are all the qualities of a saint, and at the same time a long series of handicaps which might represent in others the explanation of failure in its manifold forms.

There can be no doubt that Martin de Porres was destined by God for the honors of the altar from his earliest days. Two centuries separated the day of his death from the day of his beatification in 1837. Another century and a quarter elapsed prior to his final recognition as a saint. It is probable that Almighty God, who inspired and directed Martin during his lifetime, reserved for our own day the advantages that are to be realized by the canonization of this Dominican lay Brother.

The long struggle towards sanctity which we can clearly trace in the life of Martin de Porres began at the time of his birth. It was the year 1579. His father, a nobleman of Spain, set out for Latin America to advance his fortunes. He married a beautiful Negro woman. Once a slave she eventually obtained her freedom and became a cabaret entertainer in the capital of Panama. It was there that Don Juan de Porres of Spain fell in love with her. To prevent the news of their romance from getting back to the puritanical court of Spain he sent his mistress to Lima, Peru, bought her a house and visited her every few months. Here Martin was born December 9, 1579. He was baptized the same day. His baptismal certificate reads "father unknown".

To the disappointment of the father the child had inherited the dark skin and the characteristic features of his mother's race. Unwanted by his father he endured suffering and sorrow from his infancy. But he rose above the humble circumstances in which his mother was forced to care for him.

An exceptional child, he was destined for an exceptional career. Modest, yet outstanding in his natural attainments; poor, but appealingly generous; lively and buoyant in temperament, yet serious and deeply religious —Martin de Porres made the most of every opportunity that came to him for improving himself and helping his neighbors and friends.

His schooling was very brief. After a few years of elementary instruction, he served as an apprentice to a barber, under whom he acquired skills in medicine and surgery which in those days were exercised by those who cut hair and trimmed beards.

It was not long before this early training opened up to Martin the opportunities for practicing the spiritual and corporal works of mercy which were to form the substance of his saintly life. He became known not only as a competent, practical physician, but as a man of God, intensely interested in the welfare of his patients, combining works of charity with extraordinary personal holiness.

The design for living which was being formed within his soul found its natural expression in the religious life. In his fifteenth

15

year he applied to the monastery of the Dominican Friars in the City of Lima. His humility moved him to seek the lowest place in the convent, that of a secular tertiary. Strangely enough, it was his father who finally developed an interest in his son and demanded that the boy be given the opportunity to become a lay Brother and thus to share in the privileges of the Order. In 1603, after seven years of preparation, Martin de Porres made his religious profession. He was now a Dominican. His plan for living would henceforth become integrated with the time-honored rule of the Order of Preachers.

He would follow the promptings of virtue by dedicating himself to the works which his superiors would assign to him. It was to be expected that they would utilize his understanding of the healing arts. Martin de Porres found great joy in alleviating the sufferings of his fellow Dominicans. He joined to the practice of medicine a keen appreciation of the power of prayer and a supreme confidence in the providence of God. Like St. Thomas Aquinas, who found wisdom not only in books but at the feet of the crucifix, Martin

MARTIN NURSING THE SICK

de Porres was eager to supplement natural remedies with those which would be provided immediately by God's grace. As reports of his kindness and the seemingly miraculous cures which he wrought became widespread, the doors of the convent of the Holy Rosary were besieged with people afflicted with all manner of human ailment.

Thus we find him in one of the roles which have made him a precursor of modern social science. He was doing, in many ways, what we have since been able to carry on more extensively for the relief of human misery and the strengthening of the bonds of society. The Convent of the Holy Rosary became the forerunner of the modern medical clinic. Brother Martin became the friend of all who were suffering. Spanish, Indians, Negroes—all were equally recognized as recipients of his works of mercy. It was an indication of his sincerity and the esteem in which he was held that he was allowed to carry on his ministrations of healing within the convent whose principal purpose was to provide a home for his brothers in religion. When the scope of his services became too broad for the limited resources of the community, he was able to transfer his work to the home of his sister, just outside the city. His fundamental common sense and his unmistakable supernatural zeal gained for him not only the gratitude of those whom he befriended, but the approval and cooperation of all who came in contact with his work.

Martin was a pioneer social worker. His heart was deeply moved by the sufferings of the underprivileged of his country. If he had any fault, it was that he could not resist the urge to undertake any good work which presented itself as capable of accomplishment. He was a man of vision. He understood clearly the deeply rooted causes of the social evils of his time. He was, however, more than a humanitarian. It was the charity of Christ stirring within his soul that moved him to exhaust every possible effort to relieve the poor, the suffering, the sinful and the ignorant.

Martin lived at a time when the condition of civilization in Peru was primitive and unprogressive. Yet he was the kind of man who would not hesitate to attack seemingly insurmountable obstacles. He had a plan for the relieving of misery and suffering. It was the plan of Christ Himself: the plan of the spiritual and corporal works of mercy. His talent for organization would merit the attention of the modern social worker. Yet he never permitted his love of neighbor to become frozen in the cold water of detail and mass production. The warmth of his life, his sympathy for his suffering brethren, his profound understanding of the nature of the Church—all combined to surround his charitable ministrations with the mantle of love of God.

He was no respecter of persons, nor did he measure his efforts according to the rules of an empirically organized science. The records of what he accomplished are obviously far from complete. What we know with certainty about his benefactions reveals to us his burning desire to help his fellow men in every possible way.

There can be no doubt that Martin de Porres needed large sums of money to finance his charity to the needy. He pleaded for the poor in season and out of season. The secret of his success was his ability to touch the hearts of his benefactors. He was seldom refused, even when he asked for large

MARTIN BRINGING CHILDREN TO JESUS

donations. It has been estimated that his weekly disbursements of supplies to the needy cost in the neighborhood of two thousand dollars, a fabulous amount in 16th century Peru. The reason he was able to get it was that every one knew that whatever was given to him would be spent in its entirety for the purposes for which he begged it.

It is impossible not to see behind the successful ministrations of Martin de Porres something of the Christian charity which was still flourishing during the troublesome years following the conquest of Peru. There was inhumanity and injustice, to be sure. Yet the bloodshed and depravity that stand out in such ghastly proportions as we read the record of history were only part of the whole truth. Christian charity was still growing out of souls that had been formed in the Christian tradition. The Conquistadores were greedy for gold, and pitiless and unscrupulous in their methods of getting it. They manifested nevertheless an amazing generosity toward the victims of their ruthlessness. The human soul can be the scene of paradoxical struggles between good and evil. We must condemn social injustice where-

ever we find it. Yet we cannot be unmindful
of indications of fundamental goodness in those
who are guilty of injustice against the order of
society. Those who had conquered Peru had
been born and reared in an environment which
cherished the faith as a pearl of great price.
That they did not follow out all the implications
of the faith is painfully obvious and regrettable.
That the motivations which spring from the
faith found its way into their relations with the
helpless Incas who surrendered to them is no
less evident. They encouraged the efforts of
missionaries to bring the faith to the natives;
they were not content to think of religion
as something purely personal and irrelevant;
they did not draw from the principle of freedom of worship the implication that their
freedom to worship God in their own way was
the goal of all religious activity.

And as the Conquistadores gave large
sums of money to Martin de Porres, and to
others who besought them in the name of
Christ our Lord, they were impelled by the
reproaches of a guilty conscience no less than
by desire to bring about the improvement of
society. Today, as we reflect on the religious

background of the labors of Martin de Porres and his associates, we may ask ourselves first of all whether or not we might benefit in our own day by adopting some of their methods and seeking inspiration in their supernatural zeal. The goal of St. Martin's efforts was not the improvement of society; it was the diffusion of Christian charity. We seem to be falling into the error of thinking that the world can be transformed into a paradise by multiplying its material resources and by raising standards of living. There can be no such thing as paradise on earth. There will be suffering as long as there are human beings with human limitations. There will be social strife and friction strata of society as long as there are people who want for themselves what they see in the possession of others.

To think of remedying social ills merely by increasing material wealth and by reducing by unnatural contraception the number of those who will share it is like trying to put out a fire by throwing wood on it, and at the same time by quenching its flames with water. The wood will become charred and useless; the flames will lose their power for good as well as their destructive force

The flames which destroy our social structure can be turned into friendly fires. Christian charity is the furnace in which the hostile fires of human passions can be channeled into the spiritual and corporal works of mercy. Social evils arise in deeply rooted human drives which need to be transformed and directed, not to be destroyed. Christian charity makes the difference between the works of mercy and the expressions of vanity and selfishness which are sometimes dignified with the name of philanthropy. Only Christian charity can raise human strife to the higher level at which men will recognize in one another their brotherhood with Christ our Lord.

Again, we may ask ourselves, perhaps with greater feelings of personal and collective guilt, if there are enough people in the Church today like Martin de Porres. Certainly there were not enough like him in his own day. His voice cried out in the wilderness of a human ecclesiastical structure which had deviated too sharply from the directions set for it by the divine Founder of the Church. It is not enough to be charitable, even when we practice charity under the auspices of the Church. If

our charity today lacks truly Christian motiva-
tion, it will be even less fruitful and more
calculatingly selfish than it was among those
to whom St. Martin de Porres appealed. The
world in which we live is different from the
world in which the Spanish and Portuguese
conquistadores made their money. We live not
in a Christian world, but in a secular and pagan
world. Even as followers of Christ, we have
become conditioned in our relations with one
another in society by the effects of four
centuries of Godless thinking, and of systematic
effort to destroy the foundations of morality.
We have dangerously depleted the fund of
Christian culture which was universally prev-
alent in the Europe of the 16th century in
which the institutions of the Western Hemi-
sphere found their origins.

Our problem today is to recreate and re-
vivify the Christian environment which was so
powerful a conditioning force four centuries
ago, even among those who were attempting
to reconstruct according to their own plan the
foundations on which Christianity was divinely
established. We cannot find our way back to
the Christ whom the modern world has re-

pray for us

MARTIN IN PRAYER

jected merely by identifying ourselves with His Church. We must live as He has taught us to live. We must contribute the influence of our Christian lives to the restoration of the order of society in which grace will once more prevail against human selfishness and greed.

This is the lesson of St. Martin de Porres. He died in the sixtieth year of his life, in the forty-fifth year of his religious life, and in the thirty-sixth year of his religious profession. He followed the highest ideals; he did not shrink from the human effort and sacrifice needed to attain them. He was a man among men, big enough to dominate the prejudice against his racial origin which might have discouraged those of less sturdy character. His canonization comes at a time when the world needs to be reminded that Christ died for all men, and that none for whom Christ died can be excluded from the advantages of the society which His Father ordained in the act of creation. The race to which he brought honor must be recognized as divinely destined to play a large role in the world of years to come. Let us beseech Martin de Porres today that we who admire his achievements in the field of Christian charity may learn, as he learned, that the roots of charity lie deep in the human soul and that they have been placed there by the God of charity in whose image all men are made, whatever the color of their skin, and however they may suffer the consequences of an underprivileged human status.

THE CANONIZATION
OF
MARTIN DE PORRES

Panoramic View of St. Peter's
showing new lighting used for
the first time at the Canonization
Ceremony of St. Martin de Porres
May 6, 1962

40,000 pilgrims, 38 Cardinals and numerous Archbishops and Bishops watched Pope John solemnly declare Brother Martin de Porres a canonized Saint of the Church.

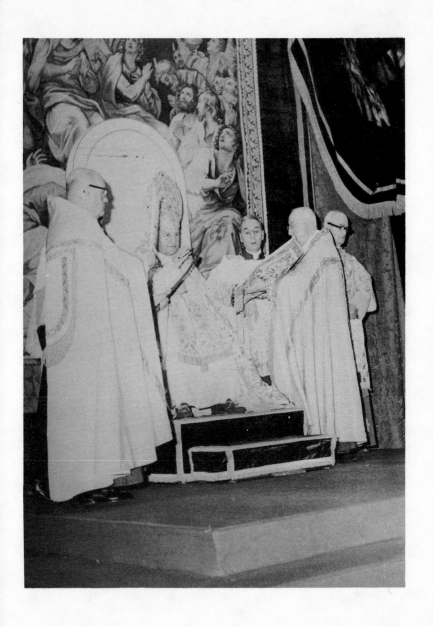

Pope John reading the decree of canonization

*The huge painting showing one of the two
miracles which were verified to support
Martin's Canonization. A twelve year old boy
from the Canary Islands, subject of one
of the miracles occupied a place of honor
close to the Papal Throne*

Portrait of St. Martin
Exhibited at the Canonization

*Head of Statue of St. Martin
in Convent of Santo Domingo
Lima, Peru*

The oldest known picture
of St. Martin de Porres

Martin	PATRON OF
De	UNIVERSAL
Porres	BROTHERHOOD

Martin de Porres was born in Lima, Peru, in 1579, less than a half century after the Spaniards discovered Peru. He was the son of Don Juan de Porres, grandee of Spain and Knight of the Order of Calatrava, and Ana Velasquez, of Abyssinian stock, a freed slave from Panama. Don Juan provided for his son although he was disappointed that the child inherited the features of his mother. In early youth the boy learned the trade of a "barber"-"doctor", quite common in that era. At the age of fifteen Martin went to work as porter and houseboy in the Dominican monastery of Lima. Nine years later, he became a Brother in the Order; from then on until his death in

1639 his duties and his predilection kept him immersed in the performance of spiritual and corporal works of mercy.

It is inevitable that the canonization of Martin de Porres should seem to have interracial significance. Newspapers commented upon the presence among the cardinals of Laurian Cardinal Rugambwa of Tanganyika, and of 350 negroes from the United States, almost one half of them Protestant. Naturally, members of the white and negro races rejoice in this honor paid to one who shares the blood of both races but we must not make the mistake of reading into the 16th century the prejudices which, unhappily, are the blight of the 20th. Martin de Porres was not exploited because of his racial inheritance and the circumstances of his birth, nor was he the butt of injustice of those more fortunately situated. The Christian society of the new continent placed no insurmountable barriers—except the artificial walls of rank and wealth—that would separate Martin from the rest of Peruvian society. In the years of Martin's youth, a developing new world gave promise of the success of the Spanish experiment in world civilization, an experiment unique in political philosophy and vibrant with spiritual values, animated by idealism such as has not been approached in ambitious design until, in the post-war world of the 20th century, our own beloved country reached out a noble, if sometimes blundering hand in order to share with the needy the blessings we ourselves enjoy.

The most important center of the Spanish colonial experiment was Lima, which, in 1579, the year of the birth of Martin de Porres, was aquiver with the mighty surge of creative activity. Provided as it is with a seaport, and removed only a little inland for better climate than the coast affords, Lima was the trading post, possessing the monopoly of all exporting and importing of all the Spanish settlements on the continent south of what is now Columbia and Venezuela. Its harbor was filled with shipping, especially in the seasons of the convoyed fleets; a stream of molten silver was being poured into the holds of those galleons, poured from the richest find of silver that the world has ever known—the mines of Potosí; Dutch and French and English pirates and corsairs and freebooters were lying off coast to plunder and steal this wealth, and Lima, in order to protect it, at least at its source, was strengthening her fortifications.

From Lima the Viceroy governed the continent; his council and the courts met there; the Archbishop of Lima watched over missionary activities and extended the parochial structure of the Church as one city after another became colonial settlements; the municipality of Lima experimented in adapting the eminently successful Spanish city forms to possessions separated from the mother country by the slow pace of vessels sailing across a vast ocean.

The formality of Spanish life had been transported along with the traditional city design: on the great square, the cathedral, the Archbishop's house, the government palaces, the court of justice, the headquarters for all contractual affairs. The streets were paved. Monasteries, convents, churches, schools were being erected, with the advice of Spain's most illustrious architect. The University of San Marcos had been founded in 1551. All the color of pageantry moved through the streets and plazas of the city to celebrate the great feasts of the Church or to welcome a dignitary of church or state arriving after his long trip from home.

The level of culture was high; the University not only educated the young but opened its doors to the academies of poets and artists and held public disputations of scholars in theology, philosophy and, occasionally, in other fields.

The silver that left the mines of Potosí came back in the form of artistic treasures and luxuries from the post-Renaissance elegance of Europe, and from the older civilizations of China, the East Indies, Arabia and other lands of the Far and Near East.

The generation of young men who had laid the foundation stones of Lima were, for the most part, aristocrats: grandees and hidalgos; their sons and grandsons, who were powerful in the time of Martin de Porres, had become, many of them, millionaires, participants in the wealth of Potosí, which was so sudden and so great as to become a strong factor in altering economic and even political life and alliances not only in Spain and her colonies but eventually in all Europe. All this change, as it affected Lima, together with the growing pains of a mixed and unresolved society, and the availability of innumerable servants of every race and degree of efficiency, might readily have made Lima a soft or dissolute community, like so many mining camps in so many other parts of the world. Lima was saved from this catastrophe by the seriousness of the undertaking and the earnest desire of men of keen intelligence and lofty dreams to create a new world built on the preservation of the aboriginal peoples and their eventual blending with those of European stock.

Though injustices abounded and various colonial propositions of Queen Isabella were being altered or discarded as impractical under unforeseen circumstances, there did exist in Lima a real and earnest and generous effort to discover a road to success in that gigantic undertaking of colonization. The Spanish and Spanish American society of Lima in the time of Martin was a serious, rather noble group of solid citizenry, influenced, naturally, by self-interest but not hardened by selfishness to the point of failing to acknowledge and—in admirable measure—to discharge the duty they owed their neighbor.

It is interesting to note that at the end of the 16th century Lima was the dwelling place of four saints and the occasional stopping place of a fifth: St. Toribio, who came from Spain to serve as Archbishop; St. Rose and St. Martin de Porres, both Lima born; Blessed John Masías, the Spanish-born Dominican who, like Martin, was a brother in the monastery of St. Dominic, and, like him, was assigned to work among the poor and needy. John Masías was Martin's constant companion and fellow worker, and their fellowship offers evidence that interracial problems did not exist in the manner we know them today. Our fifth saint in Lima was the Franciscan missionary Francis Solano, whose burning desire to convert the American Indian drove him on heroic journeys from Argentine to Mexico and along many of the bypaths in between. A society which produces saints has in it, we may be sure, the elements of spiritual health.

In spite of this gladdening picture, it would be, however, unrealistic and absurd to impute any extraordinary degree of excellence

to the commonwealth of the Lima of Martin's
day. The solution of many of its problems must
be reached as we can see, on the governmental
level, but there were others—the problems
which pierced the heart, the problems derived
from the human misery of those who had
flocked to the city in numbers greater than the
life of the city needed them or was able to
employ them. The evolution of slums was inevitable. Indians, Negroes, mestizos, and
whites settled in ghettos, for the ghetto is born
of migration. Stark hunger must have been
general in these ghettos, but, also, it must have
been generally satisfied, in some measure at
least, by the monasteries, parishes, lay confra-
ternities, by generous men and women among
the wealthy, and by others who recognized the
obligation of charity and the call of universal
brotherhood. Of these St. Martin de Porres is
the most renowned example.

When Pope John XXIII canonized Martin
de Porres, His Holiness presented him to
the world as the saint of universal brotherhood, raising him as an example of the
inspired man who recognizes himself as the
brother of the whole human race, to whom, as

to St. Paul, humanity was a unity, all the different parts of it making each other's welfare their common cause; all suffering when one part suffers, all finding pleasure when one part is treated with honor.

Universal brotherhood can never be an abstraction. It is manifested in our manner of dealing with all whom we meet on the various footpaths of daily life: in school, in business, in political affairs, in all the contacts which constitute our milieu. It is a mingling of deeds and words and thoughts. Its reality lies in the impulse of love which animates our hearts and expresses itself in every act of our existence. It knows our neighbors as children of the Eternal God, redeemed by Christ and offered eternal life through His grace. Universal brotherhood has little to do with interracialism: the man who is brother to the whole human race is scarcely aware of the lines which can separate us from one another; to him his neighbor is his brother of the royal line of Jesus Christ.

It is in Martin's daily routine that we must look for the man who understood what it is to be a neighbor, a brother, a saint. By following his footsteps through Lima and its environs we appreciate the title His Holiness chose for him: the saint of universal brotherhood. The daily trek of the devout Dominican brother earned recognition, also, from the Peruvian government, which on the 300th anniversary of his death, November 3, 1939, declared him officially the Patron and Special Protector of all works of Social Justice in Peru. In Martin's life we see universality in action. We see the links that bind together justice and charity and brotherly love.

Martin de Porres, after feeding for a spell of years the hungry who came to the monastery gate, began to go out in search of those who needed his ministrations, to carry bread to their families, to help care for the sick, to ease the lot of the afflicted, to give advice and counsel to those who were in want or danger. In the measure that his responsibilities grew weighty, he was obliged to raise funds to meet them. As a beggar, he earned distinction: $2000.00 each week, some chonicler wrote that Martin begged; $100,000 a year in whatever monetary scale is impressive. How thoroughly his supporters trusted his judgment and wisdom! And we must not omit here a tribute to those supporters and to the superiors of the Dominican Order, who were willing that Martin should make his work the career of a lifetime.

Martin not only tended the hungry, the thirsty, the sick among the poor, he also cared for the rich if he had the skill to cure their physical ills or the spiritual perception to give them the counsel they needed and craved. Martin, indeed, understood universality: the rich and the poor, the aristocrat and the dweller in the slums, the Indian, the negro and the white: all were one to this saint, who recognized only the need his brother had of him.

The problem of poverty in Lima as we have seen was aggravated, if not created, by the influx of people from the mountains into the city. There were only two possible avenues of employment open: the mines and the farms. The latter was preferable both in itself and as a base from which to instruct workers in the knowledge of God and the dogma of the Church. Martin, therefore, directed some of the money he collected into settling young men on farms and teaching them agriculture. Meanwhile he provided dowries for brides, a form of charity deep-rooted in Spanish tradition. If all this resembles a modern experiment in our fight against juvenile delinquency, so much the more likely is our fight to succeed. This was the regular procedure among the missionary orders and the diocese in Latin America. To them it would have seemed ridiculous to attempt to teach religion except as operative in a Christian way of life. We can trace this in the reconstruction of the missions of California, for example, which show the equipment which the missionaries used to teach agriculture, animal care, forestry, raising of fruits, carpentry and all other arts and crafts needed for the trades of healthy civilized life in rural sections. Martin's experiment may have been a little less complete than a mission town required, but we may be sure that it contained facilities at least for teaching agriculture, religion, and hygiene.

Some of the properties which constituted Martin's farms may have been bought with funds that Martin collected, but it is likely also that the Dominican Order owned most, if not all of them,—land assigned by the government with an eye on future missionary development,

MARTIN PLANTS ORCHARDS
TO AID THE POOR

or left to the Order in the last wills and testaments of some of Lima's settlers. At any rate, the Dominican Order was the sponsor of all of Martin's work and various superiors in their wisdom must have given him considerable leeway. Single-handed, without help or advice, Martin would have had to curtail his ambitious designs. Biographers credit him with the initiative in building hospitals, each one on the pattern of colonial hospital enclaves: homes for the sick and aged, terminal hospitals for the incurable, isolation hospitals for contagious diseases, asylums for orphans and abandoned children—small towns, in fact, in which Martin may well have turned wayward youth into the paths of virtue and made them good citizens and loving children of God. These hospitals, of which Latin America boasted scores, were supported jointly or in part by the Crown of Spain, by assistance from religious orders or dioceses, by funds of the lay confraternity which took over as volunteers for the work of the hospital and the care of the sick, and in many cases, by other private purses. There is little doubt but that Martin raised some of the money for the foundation of the hospitals wherein he labored; and to him also, biographers credit the establishment of an orphanage and school of the Holy Cross in one of the poor barrios of Lima itself.

The accomplishment of Martin de Porres during the forty-five years of his religious life was, indeed, tremendous. Wherein lay the source of his untiring labor, his constant solicitude for his fellowmen, his sublime dedication to their needs? The patient, careful, devoted work of teachers, social workers, even priests may consume many hours a day, be productive of some or all of what Martin accomplished for the hungry, the poor and the spiritually distressed, yet fall far short of or miss entirely the quality and nature of the service which raised Martin de Porres to the altar. The power of such service as Martin's is God given. As with St. Patrick, whose superhuman accomplishment in the conversion of the Gael took root in the six years he spent alone with God when as a slave Patrick tended his sheep on the mountain, so with Martin: his strength was of God. He placed all he had and all he was in the hands of God. His acts of mortification, the sleep he sacrificed to hours of prayer, his complete and utter obedience to the will of others—these were the expression of his love of God. God encouraged his total denial of self by coming to him in ecstasies and granting him extraordinary spiritual experiences. "'Eternal life is knowing thee, who art the only true God and Jesus Christ, whom thou hast sent." These words which Christ addressed to his Father on the eve of his betrayal, Martin pondered upon; he took them to heart; he meditated upon the life of Christ—not the outline map many Catholics think enough—; he entered deeply and more deeply into the knowledge of Christ and his Heavenly Father; Martin came to know God, and, like the disciples on the road to Emmaus, his heart burned within him.

This is the pattern for the teacher, the social worker, the priest who would imitate Martin de Porres. This is the pattern for all who would engage in works of social justice. This is the pattern for all conditions of people of every race and nationality and clime who would live the life of love which is Christianity.

The Church henceforth prays to Martin de Porres through her official liturgy. As mem-

MARTIN, LOVER OF ALL GOD'S CREATURES

bers of the Church our prayer is directed to him whenever the Mass of Martin de Porres is said and whenever the Church asks for the intercession of all the saints. All Catholics—those who call themselves clients of St. Martin de Porres and those who have never even heard his name, all of us are now praying to him through the life of the Mystical Body of Christ. May these prayers quicken our understanding of what is universal brotherhood in Christ and of the demands upon us in our daily lives which this knowledge makes imperative.

St. Martin de Porres, guide our faltering steps along the way of love.

NOVENA TO MARTIN DE PORRES

MARTIN, "FATHER OF THE POOR"

FIRST DAY

Saint Martin's Humility

Saint Martin imitated Our Lord Who was meek and humble of heart. There was no pride or vanity in his soul. He realized that God is our Creator and that we are but His creatures. He understood that God loves us as children and only wants us to be happy. So he had common sense enough to submit entirely to the Holy Will of God. Let us all imitate Saint Martin by humbly doing the Will of God in all things.

Prayer

O Saint Martin, ask Our Lord and His Blessed Mother to give us the grace of true humility that we may not be puffed up with foolish pride, but have sense to be contented with the gifts that God gives us. Obtain for us the light of the Holy Ghost that we may understand, as you did, that pride is a deceit of the devil and that only by doing the Will of God can we be really happy. Amen.

One Our Father. Ten Hail Marys. One Glory be to the Father.

SECOND DAY

Saint Martin's Love of God

Saint Martin's whole soul was filled with the fire of God's love. He knew that Almighty

God sent His Only Son into the world to suffer and die on the Cross for our sins. His heart was stirred with deep affection for so loving a Redeemer, and his whole life gives evidence of his sincere gratitude. May we, too, learn to love our Savior more and more and show our love by our good works.

Prayer

O Saint Martin, why are our hearts so cold and lacking in love for the Son of God, Who became a little Child for our salvation? Why are we so slow to love One Who loved us so much that He gave His life for mankind? Ask God and Our Lady of Sorrows to make us realize that the only way to happiness is by loving and serving God with all our hearts and souls. Amen.

One Our Father. Ten Hail Marys. One Glory be to the Father.

THIRD DAY

Saint Martin's Love of the Poor

Saint Martin was called "the Father of the Poor." He saw in the poor, the sick, and the dying the children of God, and he helped them in a thousand practical ways. He studied medicine so that he might know how to cure the sick. Every day he distributed alms to the poor. He built an orphanage for children.

Let us imitate the charity of Saint Martin that God may bless us as He blessed him.

Prayer

O Saint Martin, teach us to be generous with the gifts that God has given us. Make us sympathetic towards those who are suffering and afflicted. Pray to Our Redeemer and to Our Lady of Mercy that our hearts may not be hardened by sin and selfishness, but that we may always be kind and generous to our neighbors because they are the children of Our Heavenly Father. Amen.

One Our Father. Ten Hail Marys. One Glory be to the Father.

FOURTH DAY

Saint Martin's Faith

Saint Martin had a lively faith in all the teachings of the Catholic Church because he knew that it was founded by Jesus Christ, the Son of God, Who can neither deceive nor be deceived. God rewarded Saint Martin's humble faith by enlightening his mind so that he could understand the mysteries of our Holy Religion. May God give us the grace always to believe the truths which He has revealed.

Prayer

O Saint Martin, we need strong faith in God and His Holy Church, especially in these days when

69

so many people have turned against religion. Bring to a knowledge and love of the true Church the non-Catholic members of your race that they may find the way of salvation and happiness. Ask Christ and Our Lady of Good Counsel to make us faithful soldiers of Jesus Christ in life and in death. Amen.

One Our Father. Ten Hail Marys. One Glory be to the Father.

FIFTH DAY

Saint Martin's Confidence in God

Saint Martin firmly relied on the goodness and promises of God. He hoped, through the grace of God and the merits of Jesus Christ, one day to obtain an eternal reward. We know that Saint Martin's trust in God was not in vain. We, too, are confident that God will forgive us our sins if we are truly sorry and that He will give us everlasting life if we serve Him faithfully by obeying His Commandments.

Prayer

O Saint Martin, help us to have a great confidence in Almighty God. Make us understand that He is one Friend who will never desert us as long as we are true to Him. Keep us from foolishly presuming that we will be saved without doing our part, but keep us also from despair, which forgets the mercy of

God. Ask the Child Jesus and His dear Mother to
increase in our hearts faith, hope, and charity. Amen.

One Our Father. Ten Hail Marys. One Glory
be to the Father.

SIXTH DAY

Saint Martin's Devotion to Prayer

Saint Martin kept his mind and heart always lifted up to the Creator of all things. His
prayer came from the depths of his soul. It
did not come just from his lips. He naturally
turned to God to adore Him, to thank Him,
and to ask Him for help. Saint Martin prayed
with humility and perseverance, and God was
pleased to answer his prayers in miraculous
ways. He will pray for us before the Throne of
God in Heaven.

Prayer

*O Saint Martin, help us to realize that Christ
really meant what He said when He promised: "Ask,
and it shall be given you: seek, and you shall find."
Make us faithful in attending Holy Mass and other
devotions held in church. Remind us to say our daily
prayers to obtain the blessing of God. Ask the Queen
of the Most Holy Rosary to give us a share of the
treasures of the Holy Rosary. Amen.*

One Our Father. Ten Hail Marys. One Glory
be to the Father.

SEVENTH DAY

Saint Martin's Spirit of Penance

Saint Martin was a brave man. He was not afraid of hard work. He did not weakly seek for comforts as we so often do. Even though he labored so hard, he was glad to do severe penances for his sins and for the salvation of souls. If so holy a man did penances, how much more should we, who have seriously offended Almighty God by our sinfulness!

Prayer

O Saint Martin, from you we learn how to be courageous and valiant. From your life we learn to avoid idleness and self-seeking. Give us some of that spirit of penance which you had, so that we may be brave in the struggle with temptation. Ask Jesus Crucified and Mary, the Queen of Martyrs, to give us the grace to fight the good fight for victory. Amen.

One Our Father. Ten Hail Marys. One Glory be to the Father.

EIGHTH DAY

Saint Martin's Reward

Saint Martin died a holy and peaceful death. He had spent his life in doing good as a humble lay brother of the Dominican Order. But he that humbleth himself shall be exalted. Soon his heroic life became known all over the world, and Pope Gregory XVI solemnly proclaimed Martin de Porres a Blessed Servant of God. Let us rejoice that we have such a noble brother among the Saints of God in Heaven!

Prayer

O Saint Martin, you have been raised up by Almighty God to show us the way to our true home. You have given us the good example and the encouragement that we need. We now realize from your life that all we have to do to win the reward of glory is to love and serve the Best of Masters. May we ever be humble that we, too, may be exalted unto everlasting life. Amen.

One Our Father. Ten Hail Marys. One Glory be to the Father.

NINTH DAY

Saint Martin's Miracles

Saint Martin performed many miracles during his life and after his holy death. We can go to him with confidence for he will grant our petitions if they are for the good of our souls. His heart is very big, and he loves to help mankind in every way. We have only to tell him our troubles and to ask him to help us. If we do our part, we can be sure that our dear friend, Saint Martin, will do his.

MARTIN DE PORRES

Prayer

O Lord Jesus Christ, Who didst inflame the heart of Saint Martin with an ardent love of the poor and Who didst teach him the wonderful joy of true humility and the wisdom of always submitting to God's Holy Will, grant that, like him, we may be ever truly humble of heart and full of Christlike charity for suffering humanity. Amen.

One Our Father. Ten Hail Marys. One Glory be to the Father.

74

THE DAUGHTERS OF ST. PAUL

In Massachusetts:
50 St. Paul's Ave.
Boston 30, Mass.
315 Washington St.
Boston 8, Mass.
381 Dorchester St.
So. Boston 27, Mass.
325 Main St.
Fitchburg, Mass.

In New York:
78 Fort Place
Staten Island 1, N.Y.
39 Erie St.
Buffalo 2, N.Y.

In Ohio:
141 West Rayen Ave.
Youngstown 3, Ohio

In Texas:
114 East Main Plaza
San Antonio 5, Texas

In California:
827 Fifth Ave.
San Diego 1, Calif.

In Louisiana:
86 Bolton Ave.
Alexandria, La.

In Florida:
2700 Biscayne Blvd.
Miami 37, Florida

In Canada:
33 W. Notre Dame
Montreal, Canada
1063 St. Clair Ave. West
Toronto, Ontario, Canada

In England:
29 Beauchamp Place
London, S.W. 3, England

In India:
Water Field Road—Extension
Plot N. 143—Bandra

In Philippine Islands:
2650 F. B. Harrison St.
Pasay City, Philippine Islands

In Australia:
58 Abbotsford Road
Homebush N.S.W., Australia